To Sebastian   M.J.
For David and Laura   R.J.

THE FOURTH WISE MAN
Published by David C. Cook
4050 Lee Vance View
Colorado Springs, CO 80918 U.S.A.

David C. Cook Distribution Canada
55 Woodslee Avenue, Paris, Ontario, Canada N3L 3E5

David C. Cook U.K., Kingsway Communications
Eastbourne, East Sussex BN23 6NT, England

David C. Cook and the graphic circle C logo
are registered trademarks of Cook Communications Ministries.

ISBN 978-0-7814-4545-0

Original edition published in English
under the title *The Fourth Wise Man*
by Lion Hudson plc, Oxford, England.
Copyright © Lion Hudson plc 2006

Printed in China
First Edition 2007

1 2 3 4 5 6 7 8 9 10

THE FOURTH WISE MAN

Mary Joslin

Illustrated by Richard Johnson

David C Cook

THE WISE MEN stood on top of the tallest tower in the city.
They gazed up at the stars that shone in the midnight sky.
"Look! There is our special star," exclaimed the first.

"It is truly the sign that a great king has been born," declared the second.

"Then let's go and find him," pleaded the third.

"The star will lead us," agreed the fourth. Then he sighed for joy.

"It's such a beautiful star," he said. ♛

The first wise man was eager to pack all he needed for the journey.

　He went to the strong chest in the innermost room of his house. He lifted the lid and chuckled as his hoard of gold glinted in the lamplight.

　"I shall fill a box with some of my riches," he said. "That will be the perfect gift to take to a royal baby."

By evening time, the four wise men were all ready to travel.
    They watched as the sunset sky paled to grey.
    They cheered as the star appeared to fly through the night,
leaving a scattering of silver dust as it went.
    They nudged their camels and rode along to follow it.

"I brought gold," announced the first wise man. "I think it is the most suitable gift for a king."

"We have yet to choose our gifts," replied two of his companions.

"Oh dear," whispered the fourth wise man to his camel. "I didn't even think about a gift." ♛

At last they came to a town.

The fourth wise man counted up his money.

Then he went to the market, eagerly looking for something to buy.

He was so busy he accidentally bumped into one of his companions.

"Look!" said the other wise man. "I have purchased a box of the finest frankincense."

"Oh," said the fourth wise man. "Is that suitable?"

"It is perfect for a king who is faithful in prayer," came the reply.

"Oh," said the fourth wise man.

The fourth wise man left the town with a full purse but no gift.
He rode alongside the third wise man.

"Have you got something for the baby?" he asked.

"Not yet," replied the third wise man. "What I want to buy comes from far away. I asked at the market, and they said I might meet the merchants along this very road. Look! I think I can see them up ahead."

The merchants were delighted to sell some of their most expensive myrrh.

"It is ointment," explained the third wise man. "It is a gift for someone who will bring healing."

"Oh," said the fourth wise man.

After that, the fourth wise man didn't really want to talk to his companions about gifts. He was still worrying about what to do.

Then they came to a hilltop city named Jerusalem. A royal palace towered above the ordinary houses.

While the others went asking about the newborn king, the fourth wise man looked into all the shops.

"I want something for a baby," he kept asking. The only things the shopkeepers had were very plain. He fingered the coins in his purse and shook his head.

Late that night, when the shops were shut, a messenger came to where they were staying.

"Hurry! King Herod has summoned you to his palace. He has important news."

The messenger led the wise men to a richly decorated room where the king sat on his throne. Behind him stood priests in jeweled garments. Guards stood to attention, weapons at the ready.

"Listen," said the king. "There is an ancient promise that, one day, a great king will be born in Bethlehem. I want you to go and look for him there."

He leaned closer and smiled grimly. "Then come and tell me exactly where he is," he added. "I should like to go and see him myself."

The four wise men left, and followed the star to Bethlehem. As they rode into the little town, the glittering silver dust of the star's tail whirled all around it, and it hung like a jewel in the heavens.

"Excellent," said the first wise man. "The star is shining directly onto one particular house. Let's take our gifts and go inside."

The fourth wise man sat outside in the courtyard. He could hear his companions being welcomed, and he wished he could have been with them.

"I suppose I could fetch water for the camels while I wait," he said glumly.

The camels drank thirstily from the bucket of water he brought them. They lifted their heads to look haughtily at him, as if they wanted more — and faster. The man worked until his arms ached.

"One more bucketful, and that will be your lot," he said at last. 🐚

He let the bucket down and hauled it up. The water glittered in the starlight.

"Oh!" he whispered. "The special star is actually reflected in my bucket. Was anything on earth ever as lovely as this?"

Without really thinking, he rushed inside the house. "Look at this!" he cried. Then he stopped.

"Sorry," he mumbled. "I was trying to bring you a reflection. All I've done is make the floor wet." ♕

But when he looked into his bucket, the star was still there.

The smiling mother brought her baby boy to look. He clapped his hands and laughed with delight.

"That really is a very special gift!" said the mother. "It's like a little bit of heaven itself."

The fourth wise man looked up into the child's face. All at once he knew that he was looking at the king of heaven. ♛

When the next day dawned, something told the wise men that they should not go back to King Herod.

Instead they went to a different town. The market was in full swing there; children were gazing longingly at all the wonderful things there were to buy.

The fourth wise man still had money in his purse. Feeling joyful in his heart, he bought a gift for each of them.

And somehow, there was still some money left in the bottom of his purse.

"I shall buy gifts to make children smile," he said. ♜